American Boy

The Seven Paths to Honor God, Country and America

By

Chipper Chadbourne

Dedication

To the two most important men in my life, my two fathers Michael Jones and Rick Chadbourne.

Obviously from the last name, Rick Chadbourne is my biological father and was the first major male influence in my life. Unfortunately, even though I was conceived through the love of my Mom and my Dad, their marital challenges caused a breakup and an interruption to my relationship with my Dad when at a very young age for me. Fortunately it was just an interruption and not a permanent exit. My Dad was my first imprint to being a man and still is that example. He was also my first inspiration to music. He played the piano as I do and every song that I create begins on those keys. I would not be the man I am today without his DNA and obvious love and appreciation for music. He currently lives in Washington State and even though I don't see him as often as I'd like these days, every time I tickle the ivory and I play one of my songs on the piano, I can't help but think of him.

Most people are lucky to have just one Dad or father figure in their life, and I have two. My second Dad is Michael Jones. He was the step Dad that treated me like his own flesh and blood and never once made me feel any less of a son. This was the person who introduced me to the love of classic cars from the 50's. The style and artistry of cars from that era still delight me to this day. I love the cars from that day so much that my '57 Belair has become my music production company's brand and you see it in still photos as well as many of my music videos.

My step Dad also influenced my strong work ethic especially in the world of behind the camera work in movies. He taught me to be resourceful and have a never quit attitude, something that I continue to apply to this day.

The greatest thing that my step Dad contributed was to my growth as a man was his love of our country, America. My song, message and movement, *America,* was conceived from my own love of this country and the proud people that make it up and his influence contributed greatly to my great patriotic love.

I am the sum of the gifts, skills and life attitudes that was given to me by both of my Dad's. This book and the song America is dedicated to these two great men.

Acknowledgments

No book is written by itself, and so I wish to thank the following people for their wonderful support:

To my beautiful wife Mara, you share your life and being on these paths with me together, so part of the book is about you too. Thank you for your patience and steadfast commitment to this and all the projects that I pursue in life. You are my rock that keeps me grounded. You are my compass to keeping me on my paths. I love you.

To my Mom, there is a special bond that one has with their respective Mom that creates a relationship that is very strong and tells us that we are loved unconditionally. We first see the world through our Mom's eyes and that forms our belief to what a Mom is to us. Well that is about the only commonality that I have with everyone else. My Mom was a product of Hollywood in the 60"s and 70's so she gave me so much love in the form of creativity and art which is why I do what I do today. She inspired me to think and be creative and not to live a life normal to others. She inspires me to the core of my being every day of my life. I love you Mom and I wish you were still here.

To my Nana, Geraldine Baker, she showed me to follow my dreams and communicate with the world through my musical gifts and talent. She sang successfully in the Benny Goodman Band for many years she encouraged the gifts in me as well.

To my sister Holly Chadbourne, she was always an inspiration to me and was always encouraging me to follow my dreams. Holly's real gift was that she introduced me to God and Jesus and I'll always be in gratitude for her in bringing me into the fold.

Pastor Dudley, you continue to inspire me weekly. Your sermons are the basis to many of my songs and thoughts. Through you, I see the world through the eyes of our Lord Jesus. Thank you for helping me continue on my paths and continue to fuel my love for the Lord.

To David Carradine, even though you have passed on, you still live within me. You inspired me at an early age when we made the movie, *You and Me*, together. The lessons that I learned from you continue to this day. Thank you.

Thank you to Jill Colucci, singer and songwriter and Billboard Song of the Year for Wynonna Judd's song "No One Else on Earth". Jill played a prominent role in teaching me the art and skill of songwriting when I was young and those lessons carry on to today.

Thank you to all of the artists that I didn't know personally but greatly influenced my love of music and both my style as well as my message like Rod Stewart, Elton John, Rick Springfield, Lou Rawls, Little Richard, Chuck Berry, Cosby, Stills, Nash & Young, Beach Boys and of course the Beatles.

On a personal note, thank you to Florence LaRue, one of our country's great singers and founding member of the Fifth Dimension, a group still going strong and performing regularly. She as shown me that a person of faith can make it in this business and with focus and desire, inspire many generations with their music and message of love. Thank you for your friendship, your fellowship and commitment to Jesus and your divine musical gifts. You are a mentor to life.

Thank you to Johnny Britt, a multi-talented singer, songwriter, producer, trumpeter, arranger and music composer. You'll never know what you've taught me and contributed towards my development and growth in the music business.

To Debbie Holiday, the voice and attitude of an angel, and your contributions to my music brought out the meaning and message even more. I thank you for your commitment to our project and the heart that you added to my lyrics come alive.

To Roger Carter, thank you for your contribution in both playing your drums, but also working with you from your studio. Your coaching and feedback has been instrumental for me to share my music and message to the world. You are a true professional.

To Jim Connolly who was instrumental to getting this book completed, launched and to writing the foreword in this book. Thank you for your support and belief in this project, music and especially message.

And his wife, Dr. Renee Gordon, a highly successful relationship expert, busy with her own business. She put her own projects on hold just to support my cause. She has been a huge support in helping me launch this book, connect the people together to experience America for the first time and generally help me and my wife Mara in making the exposure of *America* a successful experience. Thank you for all of your help.

And last but not least, our puppies, Lucy, Blue and Sky. You bring daily joy to my heart and your puppy antics continually entertain me even when I'm too serious or wrapped up in my music. You remind me not to take myself too seriously and to enjoy life and remember to have fun too!

Praise for Chipper

"This book will put you on the high road to hope and possibilities. Do yourself a favor and teach these paths to everyone within your group of friends and family and watch the power of one take hold."

— **Patrick Snow, International Best-Selling Author of *Creating Your Own Destiny***

"Don't let those nay sayers and negative nellies read this book! Your passion for our American people comes down to people believing that as one, they can take back that power of our country. Read it now and apply it to your success!"

— **Deborah W. Ellis, CFP®, Wealth Advisor, In Demand Speaker, Consultant and Author of *Your Money and You***

"Every now and then a book comes along that provides the right perspective at the right time. Chipper Chadbourne: American Boy is one of those books. America needs a shot in the arm of pure patriotism and love of our country. Chipper provides that and shows his path to getting there for us too!"

— Dr. Michael Gross, Spiritual Healer, Transformational Coach, International Speaker, and Author of *The Spiritual Primer*

"No one addresses the importance and the power of one within our population except Chipper Chadbourne. Chipper Chadbourne: American Boy is the right book for our times. By humanizing all groups and understanding what makes them tick, this masterpiece shows how we are all equal under the Constitution and should abandon our separatist ways and join as one people, Americans. Read it, apply it and reap the benefits!"

— Dr. Renee Michelle Gordon, Relationship & Love Expert, Coach, In Demand Keynote Speaker, and Author of *Finding Your Love at Last*

"Chipper Chadbourne's message is timeless and his timing is perfect. This book needs to be in the hands of everyone who wants to unify this country once and for all"

— Arvee Robinson, Arvee Robinson International LLC, The Master Speaker Trainer, International Speaker and Author of *Speak Up, Get Clients*

"I love the way Chipper Chadbourne lays out the seven paths in a simple manner that is very easy to follow and take with us to

implement as we navigate each of our days. I think we could all improve our lives and the lives of those around us if we started each day reminding ourselves of the paths detailed in Chipper Chadbourne's book. There is not one soul on this earth who could not benefit by reading this book."

— *Steve Hornstein, Esq., CPA, CFP®*, Hornstein Law Offices, Estate Planning Attorney, Keynote Speaker and Author of *Creating Your Estate Plan*

"From child stardom to behind-the-camera work to music, Chipper Chadbourne has lived a fascinating life of ups and downs, and I love that he keeps re-inventing himself. The fact that he's devoted his artistic pursuits to spreading positivity just makes it all the more commendable. And it's not just his message; I've witnessed the positivity and generosity in his actions too."

— **Mike Malloy, Author, David Carradine: The Lost Auteur**

Chipper Chadbourne's message and music has come around just when this country needs it. His message of hope and unity and that we are all one as Americans. Read it, learn it and apply it to your own life

— Jim Connolly, Consultant, Thought Leader &
Author of iLead

*"In his book, Chipper offers the positive difference God can
make in one's life; something sorely needed in these trying times.
Through his music, Chipper propels those around him into
greater dimensions of awareness and deposits spiritual inspiration
in our hearts, minds, and souls. Anyone who knows him also
knows he lives the life he "preaches." He has a sensitive and
effective "presence" of God wherever he goes."*

— Florence LaRue; founding (and only remaining
) member of the legendary 5th Dimension,
speaker, actress, and author of "Grace in Your
second Act

CONTENTS

Foreword

In life, we are fortunate to discover a creator of great music, or a deliverer of great messages. But when you stumble upon a person who does both; create great music and deliver a great message, this is rare and should be noticed and celebrated.

When I first met Chipper, I noticed that he had a unique style about him. He calls it "normal". But being an observer of people, he is far from that description. Chipper was groomed from his early days to be an entertainer. His Mom, Nana (Geraldine Baker) and his biological dad, Rick Chadbourne all contributed and influenced his musical skill and aptitude.

Chipper was an actor at an early age of 7 which taught him the value of preparation, dedication and discipline to being in the entertainment business. These lessons from an early age educated Chipper that show business is a business and you have to be prepared no matter what!

These early lessons prepared Chipper throughout his acting career and all the way to his current musical vocation. All the while making sure that the art was at the forefront of his focus.

These "paths" in Chippers life were formed out of a need to be the best that he could be in the entertainment business. His propensity towards getting the job done and not wasting time (Path #3) continues to this day. This is probably why many music artists who have worked with him are amazed at the speed he completes a song and readies it to being published. His third path, *Just Do It*, is not just a slick tagline, its words to live by. My guess is that as a young child actor, by learning his lines and preparing for a scene quickly and just doing it, allowed him to have more play time and make his day more fun. Now I don't know if that is true, but through knowing him now, I can say that is a viable explanation to this intense habit that he's developed for himself.

But if I were to pick one path that I know directs him to be the best version of himself, it is path number one, *God, Your Higher Power*. Though this path was one of the last paths developed in him, it's become the primary or lead path in his life. All of the other paths are a strong part of him and like most patterns and beliefs, his were developed over a life time of practice. But path number one was a conscious decision that was instigated by his sister Holly. She was wise enough to know that no matter what skills and education that Chipper acquired throughout his life, that without a foundation of having a higher power to direct him, he would always be lost.

So in many ways, this direction or path has become his true path that leads him in his quest every day of his life.

Now like most humans, Chipper is flawed. And like an airplane traveling form Los Angeles to New York, the pilot will find himself off the path more times than on the path. Well Chipper is the same way. That is why path number one, *God, Your Higher Power* is so important to him and leads all of the remaining seven paths inclusive. I have noticed when Chipper is out of alignment with the other parts of his life, his immediate default action is to focus on his higher power. This has become his foundation that totally rules and guides his life.

So as much as he has such a love for his wife, his music, and the people around him, none of that happens until he is right with his higher power, God, Jesus and the Holy Spirit. As so many people explain, when God steers and guides you to your righteous path, work with, not against and all shall come to you in your life. I believe that is what I witness in that divine relationship between God and Chipper. In fact many of his songs were inspired while attending service. It may have been something that Pastor Dudley said during his sermon that became an inspiration. Or it was a voice that whispered to him, a thought of love that was the muse for Chipper to rush to his studio to begin creating a new song. Whichever it would be, it was made easier because Chipper's ability to release the ego and surrender himself to his higher power. Nothing is more beautiful than that.

So understand that this book, its message of hope to all Americans and the paths that present themselves to you is a gift from a higher power that's using Chipper to pass on the message of love, hope and fellowship. And his gift of music is to you, your path to heal and become the power of one and add to the power of being an American.

I wish you all peace, power and prosperity towards applying some of these paths to your own life and live that life towards your own divine potential.

Jim Connolly
Doctor of Philosophical Theology
Business & Marketing Expert
Thought Leader &
Friend

Introduction

I f you're an American who believes that we are all one
under the Constitution and that you believe that we
are stronger, happier and more effective as one, well
you've come to the right place. This book was written
to celebrate our oneness as Americans. So sit back, relax
and enjoy the pathways that I have experienced in my
life that I now share with you now.

Each path is both unique to its own as well as intersects
with one or more other paths. I refer to these
characteristics as paths because I see my life as a
destination and these paths are my maps to completing
my life's mission and goals. My hope is that some of the
experiences that I share with you in this book touches
your hearts and maybe makes an impact on your own
path in your own life and that it will influence how you
get to your own life's mission and goals.

The first path is *God Your Higher Power*. All of the paths
are mostly listed randomly except this path. Having God
as my higher power is the foundation of my existence

and I would not have given this path justice if I did not list it first. I didn't start out my life this way so I can appreciate the changes in my life through having a connection with a higher power. I share this with you not to convert you or claim that my decisions to be connected with a higher power is right for you, but rather share with you the contrasts of my path. When I was led by my ego during my earlier years, I was the creator of my reality. I struggled with finding peace from within myself. I blamed circumstances from outside of me most of the time. I blamed those events as the cause to my unhappiness, my confusion and my general disconnection to the world around me. Like I said at the beginning, when I finally accepted God into my life, I finally found the beginning of inner peace.

My second path is *Gratitude*. I found this path about the same time that I found God in my life. It doesn't mean that I wasn't thankful once and a while before that time. But there is a difference between being thankful occasionally and accepting gratitude each and everyday. This is the feeling of realizing that all things are possible when you truly appreciate everything unconditionally. You really know that you're in true gratitude when you accept all things and all events in your life in full appreciation, even if they may seem unpleasant or negative at the time. I give thanks every day for everything that comes my way because I accept the fact that I'll never know why seemingly negative experiences just might be a very positive one within the grand scheme of life.

In other words, I accept that I'll never know short term whether something is benefiting me now or much later. I accept and release control that I have to know now and just trust that God has a greater plan for me no matter what the particular circumstance may be. This is why I am always in gratitude, by thanking everything in life, I am attracting more of what is best for me and that I trust that my higher power will reveal the plan when that time comes.

Path number three is *Just Do It!* I've always been a doer in life. After finding a higher power I feel like I want to accomplish more and more every day. I feel drawn toward my mission and goal to use my music to bring Americans together with the understanding that we are all one under the Constitution. I am continually learning to differentiate between pushing the envelope because I can and listening to that whisper near my heart to take action. When I hear that whisper, I know that I'm taking the right path and that just doing it is all I need to do. If more people learned that life goes by quickly and if you want to fulfill your purpose on this earth, now is the only time to take action.

Path number four is *Have a Higher Purpose*. I worry when people go through life driven by a job. There is nothing wrong with putting in an honest day of work, but at the end of that journey what becomes of your purpose? My purpose starts from within me, not from outside of me. For many years I swayed from one direction to another like a boat without a rudder. I was moving but with no clear direction.

My higher purpose is to bring people together. To be more specific, to bring our country's citizens together as a message of hope and unity and celebrate our oneness as Americans as described in our Constitution of Independence, period! I hope you got chills when you read this too because your own purpose should make you do the same, get excited.

Path number five, *Don't Be Cheap*. This is not necessarily about money but more about attitude. Quality doesn't always come cheap. But quality in most cases brings greater things in life. Life is too short and precious to waste it on poor quality. In order to bring my dreams, my mission and goals to fruition, I can't waste time investing in quality that breaks down, doesn't show up or doesn't perform at its best. I believe that more people should embrace the idea of not being cheap so to reward those who are real craftsmen, perfectionists and those who are exceptional in what they do.

Give Freely without Expectations is path number six. You get more than what you give to others. Your blessings increase the more you take care of others. This path understands that the true spirit of giving is to contribute freely without expectations or reward. Many times when we do give freely, there may be benefits or rewards, but that's not the reason we give. When I give freely without expectations, it is the greatest way to show the universe that I live in a life of abundance. I truly believe that when I help another person that somehow it will come back to me ten-fold. In fact, when I give freely to someone in need, I believe that by helping that person out may be the one thing that gets them over the hump and onto their own right path. And it doesn't end there. Just maybe, when this person turns their life around, they pay if forward and do the same good for someone else too.

The last and seventh path is *Be the Authentic You*. Nothing is more important in my life then to show up as my authentic self. Some people refer to this as being the best version of themselves. I feel that I owe my creator the respect due by expressing my life in the fullest way possible.

So what does it mean to be on a path to be your authentic you?

Being your authentic you is critical for everyone. If you believe that you were created to do good in this world, that good can only be done by your authentic self. I believe to be your authentic self, you need support from your higher power to continue that being every day. It's not easy to be your authentic self, but it pays off in spades when you do.

PATH NUMBER ONE

God, Your Higher Power

E.G.O. by Chipper Chadbourne

I found out the hard way, that in life you can't always get your way;
I was edging God out, And he was the fuel to my day.

It was my E.G.O. that made me see double;
It was my E.G.O. always getting me in trouble
It was my E.G.O. making me miss the flow
It was my E.G.O. away from the higher source,
edging God out

I believe in a higher power, no longer living life in a bubble;
I have a higher source, now there's light at the end of the tunnel.

It was my E.G.O. that made me see double;
It was my E.G.O. always getting me into trouble
It was my E.G.O. making me miss the flow
It was my E.G.O. away from the higher source,
edging God out

It was my E.G.O. that made me see double;
It was my E.G.O. always getting me into trouble
It was my E.G.O. making me miss the flow
It was my E.G.O., edging God out, yea

It was my E.G.O.
It was my E.G.O., yea

E.G.O., Oh Yea!

Why is it important to have a path to God or a higher power?

A direction in life is hard to recognize in your younger years because when we are young, your ego takes over and we don't think that we need help, assistance or guidance. Maybe it was my hormones or how I understood what it's like to be a man, but when I was young I didn't see the upside to having a path that was directed by God or a higher power.

This is why I wrote the song E.G.O. which is the acronym for "Edging God Out". When we believe that we don't need help or guidance and we think we can do it on our own, we are edging God out of our life. It was my arrogance that told me that I didn't need anything else except my two strong hands and two sturdy legs to take me to wherever I choose to go and do whatever I choose to do. It got me into trouble when I thought that way when I was young and even now when it's understood that I am an adult (the vote is still out on that).

When I was young, I was at the equestrian center in Burbank where I met up with David Carradine and he pitched this movie called *You and Me*. I accepted it, moved to Hollywood and along with the money I made doing commercials proceeded to spend my money the way that I wanted to spend it.

Well not all of my money was spent on my needs. It became part of the household earnings money, which was fine. I was able to take care of everyone. But I wish I had been protected more and placed my earnings in a trust. For a while, I thought I was the adult. I didn't need anyone because I was earning my own money that took care of both my needs and my Mom's and brother's needs as well. I believed I didn't need anyone or anything. I didn't realize back then, that I was developing a strong sense of self-reliance that served me well throughout life for the most part. But ultimately, my arrogance could only take me so far. It wasn't until I was much older that I realized what I really needed was a partnership with God and not a partnership with my own self. Even to this day, I am challenged with having to rely on others, but God always pulls me back into the fold just in time.

Even when I wrote the song E.G.O., the first go-round to the lyrics was me being fanciful and totally within my own ego and not connected to my true source.

When I was reminded about the concept of ego while I was struggling with finding the right words to rhyme with caviar, limousine and high-rise, it hit me like a ton of bricks that I was doing exactly what I did as a kid, thinking that I could go it alone. I didn't need help. I didn't need support. I didn't need anyone but myself. Here I was 40 years later doing it again and making the same mistake, but with the thing that I loved most in the world (besides my wife), my music. That was one of the reasons that I wrote the song about ego because it has a message that everyone needs to hear.

Everything is easier which a relationship with God. Why do I need to go it alone? The only reason to go it alone is to feed my ego. So no more of that nonsense. I'm not perfect. I do forget these lessons. But like everyone, the more I live life, the more I get it. And I get that living with a higher power makes life fun again. I believe in a higher power, I believe in Jesus and God, I enjoy life by having a relationship this way. I have a beautiful wife and a wonderful life because of it.

I found out the hard way, that in life you can't always get your way;

I was edging God out, And he was the fuel to my day.

What are your life benefits to having God in your life?

I don't think about it as benefits as much as I think about it as blessings. I look at everything that I have in my life and I am grateful for all of it and the positive direction in the path that I take. It's all in the direction to produce positive energy within myself and in others which is why I kept my name given to me as a child, Chipper, because it's a happy name. Every time that I hear my name, I can't help but to smile and that smile may impact another person who impacts another person because of their uplifted attitude. God plays a big role in helping me positively affect the people around me.

Success is pretty much molded around positive energy and getting ahead in life. And good positive company impacts that. Good company is Jesus and God and all those folks that believe the same and that inspire me daily. These positive energy people are the only ones that I like to hang with now, if you want to shine in life in the direction that's right for you. There are a lot of people who have abused their life as an American and that's why I wrote the song America as a message of hope and love for this country. I write this music to help homeless, other people that have major problems to connect them with our country again and to add God into your life as well.

This positive energy that I communicate through my music is from my relationship with God. It usually starts off that I begin with a song or concept to a song and very quickly it becomes a Christian song or another uplifting song of similar ilk and I'm very proud that we produce music like that.

This is why I love peace and quiet within my environment. When I'm not listening to my own music, I have to turn it off and be one with my thoughts so I'm able to hear God speaking to me. I've even unhooked cable from my television monitors because I find that when I let the broadcast message in all day, even with just a few hours in the evening, I'm letting negative messages in and pushing God out. It' important that I stay present and positive to stay connected to my higher power. That is why all of my music has a powerful positive message for people to able to connect with their higher power. Our dogs are the only ones that are allowed to be disruptive because they are just being who they are as a dog and that's okay. Remember, God spelled backwards is dog. So they are okay.

I've already said it in this chapter, I'm able to pursue my dream as a producer and creator of music because of my relationship with God the true source. When my wife Mara and I attend church service, we go to be inspired by our pastor's message as well as to be lifted spiritually by the music during service. Because of my relationship with a higher power, I'm able to let go and let God speak to me during service. I'm open to a message that inspires me to write my music. Yes I may be the one that does the actual writing of the lyrics and the formulation of the sound around it, but don't fool yourself, the true message was beamed into me when I was still and in the moment, which is another benefit to having God in my life as well.

Being in the moment doesn't have to happen when I'm at church service, but because I give myself the gift of being still to listen for the message, I become very, very clear in that moment, which is why it's called, the present, because it's a gift from God.

I'm able to receive these messages at any time and at any place, it just seems to be that I receive the most when I'm being still and present while at church.

Another benefit to having God the true source in my life is that I'm never alone. There was a time in my life that I was always searching to complete me, maybe a person, an acting project or recreational drug. It wasn't until I accepted into my life a higher power, it became all that I needed.

Now I love my wife Mara and I love my life with her and if something happened that prevented us to be together, it would hurt me something awful to not be with her. At one time in my life, I would be deviated and would not be able to function. Now, as much as would miss our togetherness, with God, I'm never alone and I could continue on to pursue my mission and goal. But luckily, both Mara and I have our own relationship with God which becomes the cornerstone to loving relationship and the foundation of who we are as a couple.

I know I keep going back to it, but when my relationship goes off base as it does periodically, it is usually because of my ego. It's only when I remember to go back to our foundation of our relationship, God, that we get back on track. It's very powerful to have a home base or a center point to go back to when I get off- base within my relationship and if that's not a strong benefit to have God in your life, I don't know what else is.

So bottom line, when I know that I'm going to have a helping hand in the form of God's helping hand, I know it's going to turn out better.

How can God or your higher power put you on your correct path?

What God has done for me can be applied to anyone else's life too. I believe the music that I create is a tool to open up the conversation for everyone to accept a higher power within their own life. I don't like to force the idea on anyone. But I like to show what is possible by being an example from my own life. If I'm able to pursue my dreams of creating wonderful songs with powerful messages or to have a wonderful life partner by my side, by accepting God into your life, allows you to have it all for yourself too.

As I mentioned earlier, if you are willing to give up the ego path or what I like to call the hard path, the next step is easy. And it becomes easier with every passing day. Remember, many of us have been conditioned from a very early age to believe everything that we do, we are responsible for and no one else. Until you learn to let go of the ego, you won't ever know what I mean.

If I was able to talk to myself as a young Chipper I'd say that you follow the right path, the high-way or higher-way as in higher power, the state of mind to not look down at people, to treat them fairly, to be a caring person. And when someone does something against you, take the higher path and let go of that anger only allow love in your life. Don't judge or have an opinion with someone who leaves and let that negatively to build up. Don't do that anymore, that's not cool. Release that burden by letting go and let God. Let God co-direct your life.

Ask yourself, do you want to live your life the hard way and at the end of your life, no matter how painful and difficult it was, you said I did my way? Or would you like to share the burden with a higher power and at the conclusion of your life, you can look back and smile and say, we did it our way! It's your choice. Choose wisely.

Gratitude

Appreciation Celebration by Chipper Chadbourne

We're so glad you came; and we're on our way
Things are gonna change, welcome to the celebration

Champagne, champagne
Gonna reach your goal
Champagne, champagne
Gonna reach that high

Thank you for being here; Throughout all the years
Everything that we do; Is because of you

You've been a guiding light; Sing to your careless nights
Everything that we do; Is because of you

Champagne, champagne
Gonna reach your goal
Champagne, champagne
Gonna reach that high

Champagne, champagne
Congratulations, invitations, appreciations,
celebrations, all the occasions, decorations,

Champagne, champagne
Gonna reach your goal
Champagne, champagne
Gonna reach that high

Champagne, champagne
Gonna reach your goal
Champagne, champagne
Gonna reach that high

Why is gratitude an important path for you?

Wow, gratitude is a huge path for me and in many ways touches upon ever one of the other paths. I mentioned it before, many of these paths intersect with each other and gratitude is the one that intersects the most. The interesting characteristic about gratitude is that the more you are thankful for something, the more it tends to show up in your life, again and again.

Everyday when I have my private time with God, my true source, most of my conversation is about being in gratitude for everything in my life, my wife Mara, our home, our friends, our music colleagues, our church, our ability to create music with an important message, all these and much, much more. I never worry about money. I don't worry about running out of musical inspiration. I don't worry about life in general. I've learned that when I put my faith into a higher power and I continually express my appreciation and gratitude, it's like turning on a faucet of abundance. The more I give, the thankful I become, the more I receive. It's that simple.

Gratitude is so important because it keeps me humble in knowing that my success is due to a partnership with God. I know that by expressing my gratitude daily and more, I'm acknowledging that all things come through my higher power. It's the ultimate teamwork in the universe. With gratitude all and everything is possible.

Once in a while, I need reminding of even the little things in life are important to be grateful for and not just the grandiose events. During our time during the Covid-19 shut-in, the mayor of Los Angeles decreed that we all stay within the confines of our homes and to venture out as little as possible even limiting food shopping. Before that time, I had the ability to eat at home, drop in a favorite restaurant after my workout or meet friends and associates at a local dining establishment for a more formal meal. I wouldn't say we were spoiled but we were very fortunate to have so many options. If there is one thing I learned from not having this freedom was that I never appreciated my wife's cooking as much as I did during this time of shut-in.

I guess because of our ability to venture out into any restaurant at any time, I never had a consistent experience with my wife's culinary abilities. It seemed the more I appreciated my wife's meals, the more they continued to improve. I believe that as I showed my gratitude to her, she showed her gratitude by researching more delicious ideas for our dinners. One particular dinner consisted with the best meatloaf that I ever tasted. Now that doesn't sound like a culinary masterpiece, but let me tell you, I fancy myself a connoisseur of great American food and I've enjoyed many a meatloaf throughout my life including the ones that I've made. This was the best because of the gratitude that I showed to her and the love (another word for gratitude) that she incorporated within her meatloaf. Gratitude is the secret ingredients to not just a great meatloaf, but for life itself.

How would being on the path of gratitude help other people?

You don't have to be a connoisseur of meatloaf to understand the power of gratitude. If this is a foreign idea for you to appreciate someone else just for the sake of being appreciated, then start small. When you go to a restaurant, look at your waiter or busboy when they bring you a glass of water or a basket of bread. Look them in the eye and say, "thank you". This has nothing to do if the water is from the tap or filtered or the bread is specially heated so that your butter melts oh so slowly into your bread. No, this is all about just being grateful towards them.

Continue the trend of saying thank you at every opportunity that you can get and mean it. Be observant and watch what happens. This is not about I'll do this so I get this, no, this is about being in gratitude and that is it, period. If you benefit in any other way like people start treating you better, or you get your bread basket refilled more often, then that's great. What you'll really be experiencing is that the appreciative energy that you give out, you received tenfold the more you do it. It's not just the people that you show gratitude to start to appreciate you more, but strangers, people you haven't even meet yet that are appreciating you before you even meet. That is powerful magic and that's something that we all are capable to doing every day in our lives.

How do you express your gratitude?

I express my gratitude in multiple ways. Of course the simplest is just by saying thank you and meaning it. The energy created with a simple thank you is huge. By volunteering to do the dishes shows my wife that I appreciate the extra effort she put into our dinner preparation and that I want to assist in the cleanup. And when I go out to dinner, a healthy tip to the service staff is always a kind gesture for people who survive on monetary appreciation.

Now show my appreciation more and more through the creation of music. The song American is a fine example of what I mean. I was born and raised in America. I was born in California but had the opportunity to live in Montana. I had a love/hate relationship when I first arrived in Montana. I was in Junior High School when I first arrived. I really understood the idea of being a fish out of water. First I looked very different compared to the rest of the students. I had long straight hair and tie dye shirts and whatever a California kid would look like at the time. Not anything like a local teenager. After being beat up a few times I began the process to fitting in. Either that or my classmates got tired beating me up!

Even though at that time of moving, I wasn't very happy to the move. Looking back, it was probably one the best things that could have happened to my life. This is why by being in gratitude all of the time, you know that your higher being is always taking care of you, you just don't know what that plan is all about yet.

I got to see more of America. I got to meet the heart and soul of America. I got to know hard working people who would help a stranger as much as they would help their best friend. These were to me, real Americans. Sure, the Hollywood types were also Americans too, but I learned from traveling to the Midwest that this was called the heartland of America for a reason. This was my core inspiration to the song America. This was the message to all Americans that we are one. We are both the power of one and together we are one and that we need to celebrate that fact. Music is the cure to our separatist attitude. We need to hear this message of hope and unity and take our power back on one. What we may not realize is that through party separatism and splintering of cultures, we are more easily controlled and if you remember, the Constitution was created to empower Americans and not the people trying to control us, politicians, special interest groups, and certain corporations that fit this description. By being in gratitude and the return of our power as Americans, now we can make proper decisions to our leadership. We can proper decisions with our marketplace. We can take our power back for good. That is what it is to be an American under the Constitution and that is a great reason to celebrate!

Was there a time in your life where being on a path of gratitude not important?

Of course we all have times within our life that we let ego take front and center and gratitude take a back seat. I believe that is also part of the grand plan in looking back. The great lessons that I've learned can only be understood by understanding some basic concepts. You can't appreciate the light if you don't know the dark. It's a basic concept I know, but it's the best way to explain it and understand it.

When I was younger , this was the time that my ego got the best of me. Remember, after all, I was making my own money. I was even supporting the household too. I created this illusion that I was a man and I didn't need anyone. With a good dose of teenage hormones, the ability to make my own money and with a good over-productive ego, well you get it, no room for being in gratitude. What is so wonderful is that no matter how off base I was, no matter how far away gratitude and appreciation was, my higher power never let me down and was patient. God knew that I needed to experience the flip side first of gratitude to now appreciate its loving power again.

PATH NUMBER THREE

Just Do It!

You Can Change the World by Chipper Chadbourne

You can change the world,
You can change the world

We can change the world, We can build a better way
We can build a peaceful future, for the child that's on the way

You can change the world,
You can change the world
You can change the world tonight

You can change the world,
You can change the world
You can change the world tonight

Mother Nature's crying out, who else can you repay
Father time gives us mercy, gives us time to change

You can change the world,
You can change the world
You can change the world tonight

You can change the world,
You can change the world
You can change the world tonight

You and me, we can do it together
You and me, we can change the world

You can change the world,
You can change the world
You can change the world tonight

You can change the world,
You can change the world
You can change the world tonight

You can change the world,
You can change the world
You can change the world tonight

You can change the world,
You can change the world
You can change the world tonight

What do you mean to "just do it"?

No I'm not selling sneakers. Long before this popular tag line came into existence in our culture, it was one of my own paths. For me the path of "Just do it" means to be in action. So many people talk about taking action without ever doing it for themselves. I know, I've been accused of leaping before I look and getting myself into trouble. But looking back at my life, I see how this path of just doing it has benefited me more times than not. For me this path has been the corner stone of what I experience as action learning. I continue to develop a sense of what I need to do through my higher power. Remember, that when anyone is connected to a higher power, you are connected to pure love and pure intelligence. So you can't go wrong when you listen to that powerful inner voice that guides you throughout your day.

It sometimes looks to an outside observer that I am just a crazy person who reacts to whatever whim pops into my head. And yes, that can be the case too. Like the time my wife Mara and I purchased a Baby Grand piano from a friend of ours who needed the money more than the piano at the time. I wanted to help her out with getting her the money. Unfortunately, getting that Baby Grand to my house was looking to cost nearly as much as the piano itself. Long story short, we had four workers, I was aching to get back into my studio to complete a song so I listened to my inner voice that said, just do it, tip that puppy on its side and let's get out of here!

If you've never moved a piano before, they are extremely heavy. If you tip it with all of its weight on one leg, well I think you get the picture. I cracked the leg before we even got it out of my friend's house. What went wrong?

Yes I listened to my inner voice that told me to just do it and get this piano on the road to my home. Well that voice did not originate from my higher power but rather from my ego. I sometimes let my ego take over and make the biggest sound. This loudness will drown out my true inner voice, the one connected to my higher power, and all I hear is, go, go, go, let's get this over with so I can go finish my song.

Has this ever happened to you? Did you look back after you did something foolish or out of character and wish you had a "do-over"?

This is what life is all about to me. Its constant opportunities to listen to the right voice, your higher self or your ego, you choose. When you begin to listen to that higher self within your life, more and more, that's called wisdom. That is why wisdom is usually acquired over many years and why teenagers aren't usually referred to as "wise" because they haven't experienced enough life to develop wisdom from listening to that higher power.

On the flip side, when you stay in tune with your higher power and you hear that voice whisper out a suggestion, I honor that suggestion by taking action immediately. Hence the path of just doing it came to existence.

Why is taking action important to you?

As I just mentioned, when that message to me is truly my higher power speaking to me, I must take action because in life timing can be just as important as action and accomplishment. To put it another way, why wouldn't I take action right away. If what I've been sharing with you makes sense and the voice that I am hearing inside is God communicating directly with me, it makes sense that God is sharing this direction right this moment for a reason that I can't comprehend because my perspective is very short sighted in comparison. So I trust the information that I'm receiving. I've noticed that people who don't take immediate action let fear weave itself into their psyche. This is what we call procrastination.

First if you don't clearly hear that whisper from your higher self, it's because you're not listening for it or you haven't embraced a higher power into your life. Your ego will consistently drown out your inner voice because you've allowed it. Now you've lost trust in listening to that inner voice and you over analyze each decision so action may never take place. So in perspective, I seem to take action extremely quick.

Secondly, another reason that I take immediate action is because I've conditioned myself to do so. Never discount the ability to incorporate positive actions in your life that become a positive habit. That is why I get up in the morning and immediately take off to the gym before I have a chance to talk myself out of it. I've conditioned myself into action and to go to the gym in this way to just do it. If I would get up in the morning and sit around to think about my next actions of working out and exercising my body at the gym, I could come up with a reason every time why not to do it. So muscle memory can be a powerful ally in getting things done in your life.

So now when I hear that whisper to get into action, I've conditioned myself to do it quickly before my reasoning power or ego talks me out of it.

Now does this mean I don't make plans? Of course I do. If fact I hire people to help me manage my more important projects with me so I can complete the objective efficiently. But when I am inspired to act on a particular day, even if it is not within my scheduled plan, that will always take priority in my world.

Do you apply this taking action path into the studio with your music?

You bet I do. In fact I scare some people because they've never taken this path within their music writing before and it breaks their belief of what is possible. I typically begin my music writing as soon as I received inspiration from a higher power. When I am still and I am in great positive place, this is the best way that I tend to receive my inspiration. That is why going to service on Sunday has become my primary song writing day. I go to service, receive a message, I take that message and begin to put lyrics to it. Than by the time the lyrics are complete, the music starts forming around these words until I have a completed song. Sometimes I layer more sounds to the song and sometimes I leave it alone and keep it simple and to the point.

Regardless, I like to take action on this creation process because it was given to me at a particular time for a reason and that reason wasn't to sit on the idea and get back to it at a later time. Many artists refuse to have a sense of urgency when they get inspired. If your ideas are divinely inspired, I believe that you show your gratitude by acting on this immediately.

When God inspired me with my flagship lead song America, it was while I was at church service and the word "celebration" came to mind. I immediately began writing about celebration, but for what reason to celebrate? It wasn't until I continued to write that the celebration was directed toward our country and the people who lived within its borders. Thus the song America was born. It's a song about celebration to the fact that we live in a great country that has taken a slight turn off its right path, now needs to be adjusted. This inspiration came to me before we knew what candidates where scheduled to appear to run for the presidency, or the pandemic virus experience. This inspiration was given to me at that particular time because it was the right time. I wouldn't have known that back then. It was from a higher power that saw the need to this message of hope and unity that would be a part in reminding us all to celebrate our oneness as Americans under the constitution, not as secular groups. When you look back, we see how everything that we have done happens for a reason and benefits us. So when I get an inspiration for a song, I get to it and just do it!

Has taking massive action been a hallmark of your existence you're whole life or is it a path that you applied at a certain time of your life?

For the most part, I've always been more of a take action type person. Even as a kid, I held down acting gigs since I was seven years old. If anyone has ever worked in the film industry, there is a lot of taking action, especially if you're one of the lead characters in the film. But as I've mentioned before, I like to think that my decision making is coming more from wisdom than ego when I just do it. I have to determine when I'm taking action because I'm drawn to completion and when I'm taking action when I am just plain impatient which is from our ego. To launch this movement backed up with music with divine messages takes a lot of action and I'm learning how to apply my "just do it" attitude within a team concept that includes other people and milestones. I still do go off the path as we all do. It's allowing for that to happen and to make a correction in getting back on the path is the trick. If we let our ego take too much control, we continue on the wrong path for so long that we start believing that this is our true direction when it's not.

Just recently I wanted to test out using Facebook Live. Our team is employing a few different ways to connecting to our fans with our message and one of those ways was going to be through the use of Facebook Live. This is a perfect example where I took action quickly as I always do but lost my direction along the way.

I didn't want to make my first time on Facebook Live as a simple performance like I've seen many times before on Facebook. I wanted to make a splash for my first attempt. I spent two days setting up my back yard as the backdrop to my first live taping. Do you realize that with all of the time that I spent setting up how it looked and how impressive it was going to be compared to all of the other artists that I've seen, that I missed the point. The point was to share my music and message with our audience, that's it. What I did instead was acceptable, but I didn't even know my own songs because many of them had just been created and I didn't have time to practice them because I choose to spend my time creating a beautiful set to film in. Instead of stopping there and learning a lesson, I started performing more Facebook Live events daily, then twice a day. I'd do it outside in my backyard. I'd then do it around the Baby Grand (yes that same one that I broke the leg), then I'd do it in the studio, a place that I had sworn not to perform from. I was going down the wrong path. What I was supposed to learn was my own music, not rush out there and perform multiple times. Eventually I stopped and made my adjustment and went back on the correct path. Now I'm learning my own songs better while building up my confidence to be able to perform them again when the time is right to do so. Just do it, but be sure what the "it" is and where did you get your information, from a higher source or from your ego?

What was that time or times that caused you to apply this path to your life?

When I was younger I used to fill my days with action because I could. Once again this is when I believed that I didn't need anyone's help, I could do it alone. After all I've been working in the entertainment field since the age of seven, I believed I could do anything. So when I became a conductor on a railroad track that was for tourists during the day in the summer months, I choose to continue working throughout the evening as a cook in a restaurant. I had two strong arms and two sturdy legs and nothing could stop me. I enjoyed those times. I like being in action, even to this day. I've learned so much. Even though I put myself through college, I've learned more from just doing it than observing from the sidelines. I believe that is one of the characteristics to why my wife Mara was attracted to me because she tends to contemplate things in life and I know that she secretly wished she could just do it too.

When I purchased my 1957 Bel Air, which is the part of my Chipper Chadbourne America brand, it was mostly a pile of metal and rust. It needed a lot of work. Why would I purchase a rust bucket in the first place? It came from my higher source and I took action. What I didn't know about restoring a car of this age, I learned along the way. I didn't buy it because I had this great vision of using it to communicate my vision and feeling of America through a thing. I wish I had that sort of vision. I bought and restored it because that whisper of a voice had told me to do so. You should see the looks we get when zooming down the road. I get high fives, I get honks of approval and I don't tell my wife, but I get some sexy looks from the opposite sex when I'm stopped at a red light. its become a thing of beauty. This older vehicle is a link to a time when America was growing ever stronger due to the momentum from that victory of World War II. This was a piece of history on wheels that showed what American ingenuity was all about. It's a symbol to me of a time when American's were not so divided and that no matter what our political affiliation was, at the end of the day, under the constitution, we were all Americans. We stuck together for one thing and one thing only. We are Americans!

Even back then, when I listened to God to buy this car to restore, I didn't know all of the answers, but I didn't have to, my partner had that covered. All I had to do was to "Just do it"!

Have a Higher Purpose

The Highway by Chipper Chadbourne

Take a moment to cherish each day; accept the emotion
Just take the highway; if you think that you"r in slow
motion

I am the pathway; do you believe
I am the highway; do you believe

God is in your presence; Just read the message
God is what love is: The strength within us

I am the pathway; do you believe
I am the highway; do you believe
Forever and ever; Do you believe
I am the highway

I am the pathway, do you believe
I am the highway, do you believe

I am the highway; do you believe
Forever and ever; Do you believe

I am the highway; do you believe
I am the pathway, do you believe
I am the highway, do you believe

What is having a higher purpose path important to you?

Having a higher purpose is like the GPS to my life. We all should have a higher purpose and message to the world around us. When I say message, it means that our higher purpose leads us into action, my actions communicate a message. The message can be in the form of words, or visuals, or results and in my case, even songs. My higher purpose is to bring people together. To be more specific, to bring our country's citizens together as a message of hope and unity and celebrate our oneness as Americans as described in our Constitution of Independence.

Wow, I hope you got chills when you heard my higher purpose because it affects you too.

I'm not a politician, nor do I want to pursue that direction in order to make a difference. I believe we all are capable of celebrating our unity as Americans in our own unique way. We don't have to be within an official position to follow our path of having a higher purpose. For me, it's sharing this message through my music, video and live events to efficiently spread my message of hope and unity for all Americans.

Now don't be confused with having a higher purpose as to having a particular job. A higher purpose is the reason why you exist in this earth in the first place. It's your reason for living and being of service to yourself and others.

It's my sincere belief that many people die after they retire, not because of old age, but because of no purpose. How you make a living is not necessarily your purpose too. For some lucky few, our higher purpose is also our way of making a living by accident or design. I am very lucky that when I began my music career that it coincided with my higher purpose at the same time.

When did you discover you're higher purpose?

It's been a lifetime of clarification that has exposed my higher purpose. From an early age, I knew that I was meant to accomplish important things, but what, I didn't know. We all have that feeling in one way or another. If I could remember back when I was born, if I could put words together as I would learn years later, I probably could have told you back then, what my higher purpose was in my life.

Looking back, I can see the common thread of understanding my higher purpose. But it was more fully revealed to me when I accepted God into my life. By surrendering myself to a higher power, I switched out from my ego led life, that could not hear fully, to a life with God. When I began to attract more positivity within my life and repel negatively or what I call noise, I became more aware. You see, with God as my guide, it reduced my fears. You know fear, <u>f</u>alse <u>e</u>vidence <u>a</u>ppearing <u>r</u>eal and instead steadied my ability to see the world more clearly. Having a life with God and without fear opened up my ability to listen and tune in to my higher power.

How did it affect you once you had a higher purpose?

I don't let the small things bother me anymore. I don't let negativity hold me back. Having a higher purpose allows me to reject negative energy and stay my course.

I wake up and say to myself, "Today is a beautiful day for a song".

What do you say to others who haven't discovered their own higher purpose?

It's a very personal thing to awaken to your higher power. For some, it comes to us quickly and early in life. For others, it's much later in life that they become aware to their true path. I know for me, by accepting a higher power into my life has enabled me to let go of fear and now hear my higher purpose. That may be a way for you, the reader, to reveal your higher purpose for your life too.

I wasted time in my life searching for my true direction. As I mentioned, I was a paid successful actor in the early part of my life, transitioned over to working behind the camera for a while. I was a professional cook, the conductor of a train. I was even a landlord of an apartment building. All of these experiences that lead me to eventually question my very existence. When I asked the question, is this all there is for my life? Is this what life if meant for me? This is when I became open to accepting something that has always been within me my whole life. Something that I had ignored unintentionally, until now.

My younger brother Brandon was 16 years younger than me and I always tried to be the "big brother" that shared my worldly experiences without being too overbearing. I wasn't around that much during his formative years but he seemed to to be growing up like a fine young man. He got married to a great wife, even had a baby. Then one day his life started to take a turn for the worse. His marriage was falling apart. What purpose he once had that drove him seems to have disappeared. He even stayed with my wife Mara and I for a few months in our home and his life didn't seem that out of place. After all, young couples seem to always have their rough patches that they end up working it out.

Well that rough patch with my brother continued. I began to hear rumors that he was into drugs, more specifically heroin. He officially was divorcing his wife and his drug habit was expanding to the point that I pleaded with the family to have an intervention or get him into rehab. Everyone thought I was crazy. Well the craziness was that my worst fears came to fruition. He died in a hotel room of a heroin overdose soon thereafter. His death was such a waste of unrealized potential. The way he left us was so sad. I don't know where or when he lost his direction. I wish he would have confided with me before he got too deep into the world of drugs. He was a good kid with all the potential in the world. Alas when his path to a higher purpose became nonexistent, that became the beginning to his end.

Don't Be Cheap

Red, White & Blue by Chipper Chadbourne

All the different faces
All the beautiful places
We're all in it together
We got freedom and hope for all

America, the Red, White & Blue
United is our nation

America, this flag is for you
Through the generations

Glad you're neighbors forever,
The Red, White & Blue
We made it through together,
The Red, White & Blue

God bless America,
The Red, White & Blue

We made it to the future

America, the Red, White & Blue,
United is our nation
America, this flag's for you
Through the generations

America, the Red, White & Blue,
United is our nation
America, this flag is for you,
Through the generations

America, the Red, White & Blue,
It's in the Constitution
America, this flag's for you,
A declaration of freedom, for me and you

What does "don't be cheap" path mean to you?

The idea of being cheap is more about standard than about being a penny-pincher. In my life I've noticed people spending copious amounts of time to save a few pennies and nickels to do what? For other people, I can't answer that question as it applies to them, but I can answer that question from my perspective and observations.

I've noticed that money is a highly emotionally charged topic for most people. The majority of people give so much energy and focus on money it borderlines on worship. When cash is king (a very popular saying I heard growing up) or queen, or even emperor and even your God, this is when it's gone too far. I'm already connected to a higher power in God and Jesus. That all that I need.

When I refer to "don't be cheap" it's the path of quality and value. I have a high sense of only procuring items and services that are quality minded only. This is not a snobbery attitude and anything. It's the understanding and experience that I've witnessed throughout my life that when you purchase items or services that are branded of high quality, you tend to pay a premium price and to be on the path to being the best I believe that you have to surround yourself with the best.

What is interesting is that using and surrounding yourself with the best is not always the highest price, but if you demand the best for yourself, you will tend to reward that brand with paying premium prices. So hence the path of "don't be cheap" came about. Value is high. Quality is high and so is the finished product that it contributed to like my home, my studio, my support team, my marketing team, my artists that record and play with me, they are the best and my overall objective becomes the best too.

What have you learned about having quality in your life?

As I mentioned in a previous path that I live by a higher purpose. Many people choose their own purpose that matches their own path. But for me, my higher purpose pushes me vigorously. I don't have time to waste on redoing work or starting over and quality that doesn't match my path of "don't be cheap" will waste my time and resources each and every time.

I took the time to hire a backup singer who has some great natural gifts but in my opinion, not nearly enough industry experience and knowledge at the time I worked with her. I used her on a few songs that she did an admirable job performing, but it's when she wanted to co-write and co-produce a song, she totally missed the boat with me on understanding the point of co-producing a song.

When you co-produce and co-write a song it's usually in lieu of not being paid for your work and instead receiving a finished song as an asset that will pay you back in the long run. What is usually understood with an arrangement like this is that a version of this song will hit it big and when it makes money, everyone will enjoy the shares of victory with some healthy monetary payouts. But that is only one way to benefit from a co-produced and co-written song, the other is to write a song that both performers can use for themselves when they record and tour respectively.

Well I invested much studio and mixing time toward this project only to end up with a product that didn't help either one of us. I now realize that I have to be much more particular to who I invest in with respect to co-producing and co-writing a song. You both must be on the path of high quality and not being cheap to accomplish this task of co-producing together long term. That backup singer did nothing wrong. I should have just chargerd her for helping her with her song to make it all of her song and not help her in making it our song with the idea that we could both use it. I went this path with her to help her out with her career because I appreciated her vocal contribution to one of my songs. And even though I paid her for her time, I wanted to help her out even more. But we weren't headed on the right path as artists or as business people. So quality is not to be messed with or otherwise you can waste much time and resources as I did in this instance.

What experiences have shown you the importance of following a path of quality?

Just as I've stated before, I have a very high purpose and to be connected and active in this purpose means that I can't waste my time. God has given us all the same about of time in 24 hours in a day but he has given us the ability to have as much money as we feel worthy to have in our life. With that being true, what is more valuable? Well of course, that would be time. It is a limited community and therefore much more valuable. So I have experienced less slow-downs and delays when I invest my money into products and services that give me more time and don't waste my time. Quality tends to cost more in money, but much less in time. Do you get it yet?

As a child, I made my own money because I have been working in the entertainment business since I was seven years old. When I first gazed eyes on this BMX trail bike, I was in love. Now I could have gotten probably a similar knock-off from Sears that would have gone for half the price. But it wasn't the official BMX bike that I desired. In fact, I would have been okay if I was told to purchase the half quality Sears bicycle or walk. I was glad to walk.

I knew from my various research of this BMX trail bike that anything but the original would produce a subpar riding experience which is not what I wanted. So even as a child in my formative years, I knew the difference between quality and not. Between investing into yourself or being cheap. Don't be cheap, quite easy when you think about it.

What experience of not following quality confirmed your true path?

We all find ourselves falling off the wagon or in this instance, falling off of your path. I too have been tempted to not following my path of "don't be cheap" as well.

You have to be real now. Sometimes cash flow can be tight and you have to choose with price first and not quality first. I would start in knowing that I was cash challenged at the time, aka barely broke, and my attitude going into that situation began that way. By the way, do you notice how we can become real creative with our stories when we are avoiding the real issues at hand, like being broke? I've done this too. I've come up with justification stories that when I look back, I can just only smile.

When my team and I were planning for the launch of my flagship song and message to our country, America, we talked about how would we do this. Part of the team suggested that we do this at my and Mara, my wife's, home. Now we have a wonderful home that we love. It's very comfortable for us and was designed to our taste in mind, but to have a celebration to the launch of America was a stretch.

I listened to the arguments to why we should host in at our home, slowly being convinced it was the direction to go until I heard the voice inside say, "Don't be cheap!"

Wow, it was a wake-up call, a reminder of one of my correct paths to not waste time doing something half-assed just to save a few bucks. The celebration would have been at best, okay. But with such an important message to the American people, doing it in this way would not have been as impactful.

When the Covid-19 situation caused us to re-evaluate our event again, we struggled with how and where are we going to hold our celebration and launch of America the song, the album and the movement. Even if the county and city of Los Angeles allowed for public gatherings, would people show up or would they be scared to venture out of their homes to surround themselves with other people?

The idea of having a virtual celebration and launch seemed to be more a reality. The venue that we had a deposit to hold our event date, would be described as a very opulent and over the top to not have live guests present. So the idea of having our virtual event at a simpler venue like a warehouse was a cheaper option.

Once again, that nagging voice from within was beginning to bug me and I heard the voice say, "Don't be cheap", do it up correctly or don't do it at all! Okay, okay, I get it. Let's go back to our original venue and present to them this new scaled down option. Also, we decided to lead our celebration with this now being a charitable event to benefit the Wounded Warriors Project and Widow's, Orphan's & Disabled Firefighter's Fund. Our original venue could see we were trying to work with them and make it a win-win event for everyone involved, our charities, our raving fans and future fans, our venue and especially for all of the virtual guests who we touch with our message of hope and unity. Our venue wanted in and presented a substantially lower price in order for us to continue staying with them. This highly important event all was falling in place because I listened to my inner voice tell me, "Don't be cheap", and we didn't.

PATH NUMBER SIX

Give Freely without Expectations

Bridge of Faith by Chipper Chadbourne

I will be your stepping stone, a bridge of life, faith and hope
On this stone we will stand; I will be your comfort hand

I will be your stepping stone; walk this path you will grow
You will never be alone; my heart is what you own

With a bridge of faith, fill our hearts with gospel
With a bridge of faith, our faith will always be there
With a bridge of faith, fill our hearts with laughter
With a bridge of faith, we will take your higher

Gonna be there where you are; step by step the bridge will never fall
Come with me through it all; I have loved you from the start

We will never fall apart; I'm gonna be there every day
Feeling your sweet embrace; we will get through it all

With a bridge of faith, fill our hearts with gospel
With a bridge of faith, our faith will always be there
With a bridge of faith, fill our hearts with laughter
With a bridge of faith, we will take your higher

With a bridge of faith, fill our hearts with gospel
With a bridge of faith, our faith will always be there
With a bridge of faith, fill our hearts with laughter
With a bridge of faith, we will take your higher

With a bridge of faith, fill our hearts with gospel
With a bridge of faith, our faith will always be there
With a bridge of faith, fill our hearts with laughter
With a bridge of faith, we will take your higher

With a bridge of faith, fill our hearts with gospel
With a bridge of faith, our faith will always be there
With a bridge of faith, fill our hearts with laughter
With a bridge of faith, we will take your higher

What does following a path of giving freely mean to you?

You are getting more that you you give, your blessing increase the more you take care of others.

The song The Highway is about the higher power. Realize that what you put out to others comes back to you even more. Some call that karma. I call that just giving freely.

Some performers have a scarcity attitude because of no connection to a higher power. They can't be happy with another person's success and want to help you freely because they focus on scarcity instead of abundance. Also, when I say freely, I don't mean if they are paid or not. When I work with a professional, I will either pay for their time or cut them into the ownership of the song for them to benefit later. What I mean by freely is that when they are connected to a higher power, they want for nothing. They understand that to have a relationship with God and that God will always provide. That is more of an abundant attitude. No worry that you won't get yours and that by giving freely to help elevate another artist, you'll be rewarded ten-fold or more.

It's not about giving to expect and that you'll give only because you'll get back in return ten-fold or more. That is once again is a scarcity attitude. All of my paths all intersect, to give freely means that you've embrace a higher power that gives you abundance in your life.

So even though I'll bump into other artist who'll claim to have accepted a higher power or God and Jesus into their life, yet they haven't understood what that means because they still let money, fame and ego run their lives. One particular talented artist that I work with was just like this. He claimed to have accepted God into his life and that is one of the reasons that I opened up my heart and home to him without hesitation. We proceeded to create together. I paid him well for his efforts and because I respected his talents and resume, I never questioned his intent. I even had him assist me on my flagship song, the tune that really reflected my values and beliefs about our country. In a nut shell, I trusted completely because I thought we shared a common relationship with a higher source.

Now full disclosure, I've been told that I'm somewhat a savant when it comes to writing a song and completing it in blazing speed. I have music in my blood from my family's background, especially my Nanna, who sang with the Benny Goodman Orchestra for many years. But I don't consider myself a pure vocalist but more of performer and song messenger. So when my fellow artist whom I trusted professionally put the key to my lead song in a cord just out of my vocal reach, that is when it became apparent. He has a much better vocal range than I. Because he did not embrace his higher power, he missed the opportunity to place the cords where we could both sing it together and share the glory. Because it was written from a place of scarcity and not abundance, we'll never know if this would have been a bigger hit because our voices would have merged as one and would have illustrated the message of unity, the message that my lead song, American is all about.

Almost as quick as I accepted him into my life, he turned into a scarcity entity. Now on one hand he accepted the Lord and Savior into his life but seemed to have an exception when it came to business and money. When I accepted a higher power, I accept fully and completely. No separate rules when doing business as opposed to building relationships. Life is life, not separated into a work life and a social or family life. I'll quote a friend of mine, Dr. Renee Gordon, "what you do in one part of life, you do in all parts of your life." You've conditioned yourself to be a certain way and that is reflected everywhere.

All I can do is be my authentic self, have a relationship with my higher power and to give freely without expectations

Why don't you expect something back when you give freely?

As I said earlier, when you give freely without anything back in return, you are living an abundant life. The expression that I share with my wife Mara is , "We have more blessings around the corner".

When you expect something in return you are communicating to your inner self and to God that you never planned to give freely in the first place. The act of giving never has a condition placed upon it.

One of my workers who helped me on my latest album, was going through a rough patch and needed a place to stay. I put him up in a clean, quality local hotel while he was working for me. It wasn't part of his pay. He was paid his full amount as an assistant to me on this music project. Yes, I could have easily had his room and board as his payment, but that wasn't my intention. I wanted to help this young guy get back on his feet and become self-sufficient after his job with me was complete.

We know when we give freely. If we are present with ourselves, we can hear that voice within us clearing its voice and saying, "are you sure your intentions are pure?"

I truly believe that we have more and more blessings around the corner. Why not help someone now and show that I truly believe that more blessings are on the way.

In your life, has someone helped you in a way that has put you on a path of paying it forward?

Of course, we have all had angels in our life. Even when we need help, it does not always mean you have to be in dire straits to need a helping hand.

I give $20 at a time when I see a homeless person in the street. This is why I do that. I believe that there is more from where that came from. There are more blessings around the corner.

I don't write about this to impress anyone, these actions are my life. I know it seems we are becoming a society with cameras taping us all of the time. The reality is that I would feel for the person following me around and watching my every move. In general, my life only means what I want it to mean. When I give, I give because it's right. I've been blessed and I continue to be blessed every day so when I experience a person sitting on the side of a 7-11 convenience store hoping for some pocket change, I bless him with $20 so maybe he or she might get a decent meal.

When I have one of those days, you know what I'm talking about, when I'm acting like an ass. I immediately see the results of my day changing. I immediately recognize that I am the creator of my day. I am responsible for my actions and I am also responsible for my abundance. There are more blessings around the corner and the more I give, the more I experience more blessings. When I'm experiencing blessings, I'm what I call, being in the flow. When I was working on my song E.G.O., I mentioned how rough it was to write in the beginning because I wasn't in the flow. I wasn't giving freely without expecting something in return. When I was in my ego, it blocks my flow. But once I turn on the giving freely, it opens up like a kinked up water hose. Once the kink is removed, the water flows freely. The ego is the kink in the hose. Remove the ego and the rest just flows. Giving freely unkinks your blessings.

Even when I went to the studio and the producers are hearing the changes to the song, they all looked at me like they had just gotten a sniff of some good smelly ripe cheese. It wasn't until they experienced the flow of the hook of my song and understood that E.G.O. meant the ego is Edging God Out, they went from frantic to fan within an instant. Giving freely unkinks your blessings every time.

What is your philosophy to giving and how would you influence others to think the same?

I've been saying all along, my philosophy to giving is that I have blessings right around the corner. I would like to believe that all the giving that I have done throughout my life has positively affected the people around me.

I'd like to believe that my wife Mara has been touched by my generosity to others going through a challenging time in their life. I'd like to believe that this core belief that I hold continues to rub off on her too. The idea that it's better to give than receive is not just a popular saying that gets an "ahhhh" from those who overhear it being said. It has to come from your authentic you and your connection with God the true source.

I believe that the recipients of my generosity have done the same for other people as well and have paid it forward. I use the term in our movement that we are stronger together with the phrase, "The Power of One", meaning it starts with me, then to you, then to the next one, then the same again and again. The Power of One is perfectly illustrated by paying it forward. I know that giving a homeless person $20 is not going to solve his or her general problem. But it may feed him or her a nutritious meal right this moment. And that proper fueling of nutrition gave them the energy to take the next step in turning around their life. And this cycle continues until that homeless person is changing their life and slips a different homeless person $20 to make the positive cycle continue.

The Power of One is all about doing the next right thing that you have control over doing. It doesn't solve the Covad-19 pandemic. It doesn't cure cancer. But it does make a difference. And when enough people take action and pay it forward, we all become an unbeatable force of nature.

So my philosophy that many blessing are just around the corner can be your philosophy too, if you choose.

PATH NUMBER SEVEN

Be the Authentic You

On My Mind by Chipper Chadbourne

On my mind

On my mind, on my mind
On my mind, on my mind

Jesus I think about you all day long, cause you're on my mind
At times like this kaleidoscope, your words say what I need to know

I've been living life in a hurry, take it slow no need to hurry
Cause you're on my mind

Jesus on my mind, on my mind
on my mind, on my mind

My mind was in a million pieces, when I couldn't think of you
I was stranded on an island, now I'm safely flying most of all 'cause of you

81

'Cause you're on my mind, on my mind
On my mind, on my mind

On my mind, can't see your face
Through your embrace, you hear my voice,
inside of my heart there is a voice and it goes like this,
You and me we do it together
You and me we do it together

You and me we do it forever
You and me we do it forever

'Cause you're on my mind
You're on my mind

You and me we do it together
You and me we do it together

'Cause you're on my mind
You're on my mind

What does it mean to be on a path to be your authentic you?

Being your authentic you is critical for everyone. If you believe that you were created to do good in this world, that good can only be done by your authentic self. I believe to be your authentic self, you need support from your higher power to continue that being every day. It's not easy to be your authentic self.

Think of Jesus, he was crucified for being his authentic self. His mission and goal on this planet was huge, but in order to compete it, his life was put on the line. So I'm sure that wasn't easy for even Jesus to have experienced, being punished for being the best version of himself. He could have been a tad bit less authentic so he could stick around longer. But would he have been as impactful on the world and on history if he had not gone all in?

Now being authentic for you and it doesn't mean we are at risk to being crucified for being real. But it will present interesting challenges and reward you with beautiful results.

One guy that records in one of the studios that I work with has been recording the same song over and over. He's had at least five different renditions of the same song. Because he has no connection with a higher power and he has no higher purpose, he can't recognize his authentic self when recording. Having that inner voice that supports you and tells you, "Yes, this is the right path for me", is being the authentic you.

Sadly, he's a real good singer.

I've created imperfections when I write music. In one of my songs, I say "walk" three times within a structure rule and I don't care because the message is there. I am authentic with myself enough to continue on with that song because I am confident that the message will inspire the listener and they won't care about the structure rule either.

So If I can do that, this guy should be able to pick his authentic version that represents him and the message that he wants to share to his fans.

How do you gauge that you are being on your own path of being authentic?

One way that I know that I'm on my path of being authentic is shown by my results. Much like when you have a headache, the symptom of your head throbbing is a symptom or result of the bigger cause of being dehydrated. And after drinking a couple of glasses of good quality water, the symptoms of having a headache go away.

Well the results or symptom of my day being productive, helping someone, showing appreciation to my wife, being in gratitude to my health, my home, my life, then I'm following my path of being authentic to me.

If my day is falling apart, my relationship with my wife less than desired, my music is off key and generally I feel like poop, well, I'm not being my authentic self. It's that easy. Nothing happens outside of me that didn't happen first from inside of me first. I control the dialogue of my life by the relationship with my higher power, my life purpose, and my gratitude.

Being your authentic self applies to many situations. When you are not being your authentic self, usually those are times that your regret. My Mom remarried after her previous union that produced a step brother who was two years older than me, his name was Christopher. Like older brothers do, he has always beating up on me and I was always trying to get back at him by telling on him. It was a symbiotic relationship of sorts but it worked for us. One day Christopher and his friends were in the space above the garage shooting off fireworks and more. Well the more I discovered what was really going on was that they had a hand gun from his friends home and they were using the fireworks to cover up shooting off the gun into the canyon below. When I climbed up to see what they were doing and saw the hand gun, it was a perfect opportunity to tell on him in a major way. But this time was different. His friend was their too. I didn't want to look like a snitch even though I knew that was not safe for them to play with a gun. So I promised not to tell. Went down the ladder and back into the house to watch television since these were not my friends and they made it clear I wasn't welcome. I was hanging out with my Mom when we both heard, "Chris has been shot!" The ambulance was called and we quickly rushed to my brother's aid. His best friend had accidentally shot him in the chest with a mortal wound. There was nothing the paramedics could do. I wish I had stuck to my authentic self and had told on him.

Is being on your path of being authentic also mean being the best version of yourself?

You cannot be the best version of yourself if you are not being authentic. Everyday is a challenge to stay on the positive path and deal with the ever present negativity that can sneak in when you least suspect it.

I'm always challenging my skills, my capabilities and my results. I know that God created me as unique and different as a snowflake. I spent some time in Montana, a totally different environment to Hollywood California. When you look at piles of snow pushed to the side of the road by the many snow plows, you don't realize the many unique formed and shapes of snowflakes that make up a hill of snow. But make no mistake, each snowflake is different and God created me very different as well.

I don't believe in comparing myself to others including other performers, writers or music producers. By doing so, I immediately reject my uniqueness that God made for me and me alone. I've mentioned that I have a gift to take an inspired idea and construct a song very quickly. I have this gift to stay very focused and just get it done. I've helped other producers speed up their delivery time by teaching them my gift and the process that I use to create. I don't accept that I'm good enough in that one part of my life and to work on another "weaker" part of my life. No, to be the best version that I can be, I have to continue improving my gift and take it to another level, maybe to a place that I can't even imagine.

With that being said, I'm always challenged to growing my relationships around me. I know it's a life-long challenge being misunderstood, but I surround myself with people that truly understand me and help me grow those relationships that don't quite get me yet. It took me 19 years to finally marry my lovely wife Mara. She gets me more than anyone out there but I'm always challenged in sharing how much she means to me in a way that she appreciates. Everyday I work on being the best version of myself for Mara and it begins with being in gratitude. I know that it sounds simple in being thankful for Mara everyday in order to make me the best version of myself. Somedays I fall into the ego part of me and my world attacks me including my world of Mara. Those days can be very difficult until I realize that I am the creator of my authentic self and I can reverse that outside control to the optimum inside first level. When my relationships go off- base, that is when I need to lean on God more so I can be the best relationship version of myself. A lifelong pursuit but a worthwhile one for me.

Why is it important to be the best version of yourself?

Just like when I give freely without anything in return, I believe that I need to continuously pursue the best version of myself without anything in return. To continually be my best version is to honor God. He gave me all of the basic gifts to point me towards being me. Now it's my job to continue the work that God put into me and honor the great job that was done.

By being my best version I'm paying it forward everyday. I may be inspiring the next generation or I may be inspiring an artist who is kicking off their career later in life much like I did.

I've done a lot of things in life, I've been a lead actor in a major motion picture, television commercials, developed methods to shoot aerial shots from a helicopter (pre-drone era), worked behind the scenes in other movies, restaurant cook, even a conductor of a tourist train that traveled from Nevada City and Virginia City in Montana. But I've always had my music since I was young. My Nanna sang with the Bennie Goodman Orchestra. My Mom was a great actress in her own right. I have cousins who continue to make music as well. So

I guess I've always had music and entertainment in my DNA, now, to be all I can be, to be the best version of me, I needed to take action and develop my musical potential while communicating a message of hope and unity to our country that we are all one under our constitution, as Americans.

How does believing in a higher power, in your case, God and Jesus, apply to your path of being your authentic self?

Being my authentic self is honoring God and Jesus. I believe that I was put on our earth, in our country at this time in history for a reason. I believe that by being my authentic self, developing those gifts given to me by God and Jesus and following my mission and goals are all part of my path.

I can't believe that I've been given all of these talents and skills to not use them for a higher purpose. And why now you ask? Why do all of those dormant yearnings come alive now? Why are our country's citizens at major odds against one another? Why, why, why?

Rather than ask the question why, how about "what". What should I do about using all of these natural gifts?

What message should I share with the American public? What do I need to do to get started? Well I did and I am and I'm being the best version of myself through the support of my higher power.

Every time I'd return home from church service, I needed to act upon the inspiration that Pastor Dudley laid down before me. I needed to continue being the best version of myself and take action creating a song from the message that I just heard. This is how I continue being my authentic self. Just like my song E.G.O., I need to remind myself daily not to Edge God Out. So when I include God in my life as my co-creator and partner, I can't help by be my authentic self.

Is it easy to continually be your authentic self? No, but as Stevie Wonder said, "Nothing great comes easy."

America by Chipper Chadbourne

America, America

We gonna celebrate, we're gonna celebrate tonight

We gonna celebrate, we're gonna celebrate tonight

America

Celebrate tonight

It's gonna be alright, grab a friend

Shine your light

Grab a friend for the whole world to see, be all you can be

Raise your head up high, with pride, America , America

Faith and love for our country, time to celebrate our love

Celebrate tonight, celebrate tonight, celebrate tonight

This is a special night to remember, how we all came together forever

For the whole world to see, we are all family

America, America

Faith and love for our country, time to celebrate our love,

Celebrate our love, celebrate tonight

America , America, Celebrate our love

America, Celebrate our love,

The red, white and blue
The red, white and blue
The red, wheat ad blue

America, celebrate our love
America celebrate our love
America celebrate our love

America celebrate tonight
America celebrate tonight

Let's celebrate

Lyrics to Chipper's Other Songs:

Listen to Chipper's other meaningful songs that can be found on his website, www.ChipperChadbourne.com

Wake up

I woke up to a beautiful day,
Sun's out, it's God's Sunday

I woke up to a beautiful day,
Sun's out, it's God's Sunday

Praise Hallelujah
Praise Hallelujah

God's love is contagious,
God's love is kind
God's love will get you through the hardest time

Love isn't suffering all the time,
It's in your heart and your mind

I woke up to a beautiful day,
Sun's out, it's God's Sunday

I woke up to a beautiful day,

Sun's out, it's God's Sunday

Praise Hallelujah
Praise Hallelujah

God's love is contagious,
God's love is kind
God's love will get you through the hardest time

Love isn't suffering all the time,
It's in your heart and your mind

I woke up to a beautiful day,
Sun's out, it's God's Sunday

I woke up to a beautiful day,
Sun's out, it's God's Sunday

Praise Hallelujah
Praise Hallelujah

Your love is patient,
Your love is patient
Your love is kind,
Your love is kind

Your love is patient,
Your love is patient

Your love is kind,
Your love is kind

I woke up to a beautiful day,
Sun's out, it's God's Sunday

I woke up to a beautiful day,
Sun's out, it's God's Sunday

Praise Hallelujah
Praise Hallelujah

I woke up to a beautiful day,
Sun's out, it's God's Sunday

I woke up to a beautiful day,
Sun's out, it's God's Sunday

Praise Hallelujah
Praise Hallelujah
Compassion Walk

It shines like a diamond

It shines like a diamond
It shines like a diamond

It shines like a diamond
It shines like a diamond

Your walk matches your talk
Your light shines so bright

It shines like a diamond
It shines like a diamond

It shines like a diamond
It shines like a diamond

You work hard at pleasin,'
Your grace makes the angel's sing
You are the power of one,
You are the story of perfection

It shines like a diamond
It shines like a diamond

It shines like a diamond
It shines like a diamond

It shines like a diamond
It shines like a diamond

It shines like a diamond
It shines like a diamond

Faith and love, your walk matches your talk

You let them see your good deeds,
You let it shine, shine, shine

It shines like a diamond
It shines like a diamond

It shines like a diamond
It shines like a diamond

It shines like a diamond
It shines like a diamond

It shines like a diamond
It shines like a diamond

You are the power of one,
I am the power of one

You are the power of one,
I am the power of one

You are the power of one,
I am the power of one

It shines like a diamond
It shines like a diamond

It shines like a diamond

It shines like a diamond

It shines like a diamond
It shines like a diamond

It shines like a diamond
It shines like a diamond
You're A Star

You're a Star, realign

You're a star, guiding light

Your a star, energize
Your a star, in my eyes

Climb the ladder of fortune and fame
Your dreams get shattered but forget your name
What is it that guides you, had your heart been pure
Do you want to go viral, what is the cure

You're a Star, realign
You're a star, guiding light

Your a star, energize
Your a star, in my eyes

I could be your energy, it's all in your frequency
Your spirit is the light turned on, a mirror away from me

A mirror away from me
My life will be a masterpiece, the light your see has set me free

You're a Star, realign
You're a star, guiding light

Your a star, energize
Your a star, in my eyes

I could be your energy, it's all in your frequency
Where are you going, where is the turn

You're a Star, realign
You're a star, guiding light

Your a star, energize
Your a star, in my eyes

You're a Star, realign
You're a star, guiding light

Your a star, energize
Your a star, in my eyes
On My Way

I'm so glad you called baby,
I want to be with you
Try'n to take a road trip baby,
It's got my fire with you, tonight

I'm on my way

I know you're worried,
When I'm away
You know I'll be there,
Everyday

I'm so glad you called baby,
I want to be with you
Try'n to take a road trip baby,
I got my fire with you, tonight
I'm on my way

Say I came to see you, tonight
You look so good
We would never stay up hun'
Baby you'd love me like you should

I'm so glad you called baby,
I want to be with you
Try'n to take a road trip baby,
I got my fire with you, tonight

I'm on my way

I'm so glad you called baby,
I want to be with you

Try'n to take a road trip baby,
I got my fire with you, tonight

I'm on my way, baby
I couldn't stay away

I'm on my way, baby
I'm on my way, tonight

I'm on my way
I'm on my way
Tonight

I'm on my way, baby
I couldn't stay away

I'm on my way, baby,
Gonna see ya tonight

About the America Movement

We're Creating a Movement!

And you are the main part of this movement

Chipper Chadbourne has witnessed the growing trend of proud Americans battle each other over trivial ideology and party preferences and is afraid that it will hurt the spirit of our country beyond repair.

Join Chipper and many others in this celebration/movement. Chipper believes that music can be the tool to heal a battered national psyche and remind our country that we are all one in the same, Americans!

Go to www.ChipperChadbourne.com and join the Chipper Chadbourne inner circle of Americans wanting to celebrate our oneness as Americans under the Constitution. We'll keep you updated to the latest news in our quest to restore our love and hope for our country as well as live dates and performances.

Join the Power of One!

Chipper Chadbourne Bio

First and foremost, Chipper Chadbourne is a proud American. His song *America* represents his wish and desire that we as Americans celebrate our oneness as Americans and not fall into the ravages of one political party or another, one culture or another, one select group or another, but one as Americans. Only this attitude of gratefulness and love for our Constitution and our country, our common identity and cause, should be our focus.

In a sense, this is all about self-empowerment to remind all of us what a great country that we live in and nothing will tear us apart. In short, he loves America.

Chipper has been in the entertainment business his whole life. His claim to fame was during the 70's, co-starring with David Carradine in the movie You and Me. He has also been in many other productions and commercials on television as well. He grew up in the industry with many family members who mentored him in both acting, music and performing.

Chipper's main purpose is to change the world and remind us all that we are best united than apart and that we can do this together; one note, one song and one concert at a time.

You are the power of one!

Book Chipper Now

Chipper would love to perform at your next corporate event, family get together, church function or any opportunity to celebrate as fellow Americans.

Go to www.chipperchadbourne.com/book-now.html

Fill in the provided contact form and one of our friendly representatives will reach back to you immediately.

Or send us a direct email at chipper@chipperchadbourne.com

Made in the USA
Columbia, SC
02 August 2020

14469949R00067